Beyond
Imposter Syndrome

Proven strategies for building confidence
and finally feeling 'good enough'

Margaret Collins

Published by Margaret Collins

Edited by Deborah Taylor, Book-Launch Your Business

Cover by Mohamed Mustafa

Typesetting and book design by www.candescentpress.co.uk

Free test: Do you have Imposter Syndrome?

Perhaps you decided to look inside this book because you were drawn to the title or maybe because you already know of the imposter phenomenon and how it leads capable, talented people to feel they are not good enough, especially at times when they should be feeling confident in their abilities and skills.

It's also possible that you've heard of something called "Imposter Syndrome" and you're intrigued but not sure whether this affects you or explains what you feel. Imposter syndrome is not a diagnosable medical or psychological condition so there isn't a definitive test but there are a set questions you can answer that will give you much greater insight into whether or how you are affected by impostor feelings in your daily life.

You can access your copy of these questions on my website at https://MargaretCollins.com/ImposterQuestions. To see whether you have some of the typical signs of feeling like an imposter, do visit and download your copy today.

I hope you enjoy reading the rest of this book. It will explain where imposter feelings can come from and also practical steps that allow you to successfully move beyond your imposter feelings, to be comfortable being yourself and to feel good enough for whatever life brings you.

Acknowledgements

As I write this book, I want to thank the many people who have encouraged and supported me in my work and my learning.

I particularly want to thank the many, many participants in my workshops who have courageously explored their imposter feelings and shared their brave and creative solutions with me over many years. This means that the wisdom shared in this book is as much based on practical experience as it is on "book learning" and academic research, a happy marriage indeed!

Dedication

I am inspired by many writers and, though it took me a little while to completely own this, the following quotation from Marianne Williamson has always inspired me – and in fact continues to inspire me... May it encourage you to let your light shine, not that you might stand higher (though you might) but so that others may feel they have permission to do likewise.

"Our deepest fear is not that we are inadequate. Our deepest fear is that we are powerful beyond measure. It is our light, not our darkness that most frightens us. We ask ourselves, Who am I to be brilliant, gorgeous, talented, and fabulous? Actually, who are you not to be? You are a child of God. Your playing small does not serve the world. There is nothing enlightened about shrinking so that other people will not feel insecure around you. We are all meant to shine, as children do. We were born to make manifest the glory of God that is within us. It is not just in some of us; it is in everyone and as we let our own light shine, we unconsciously give others permission to do the same. As we are liberated from our own fear, our presence automatically liberates others."

Marianne Williamson

Contents

FOREWORD

Foreword

I remember talking to a woman in one of my workshops. She was in her forties, bright and energetic. I knew her professionally as a leader in her field: a frequently-published author who was trusted by her colleagues and was sought out and acknowledged internationally as an expert in her subject area. In recognition of her success she had recently been appointed Professor at a leading UK university. Anyone on the outside looking at this person saw a highly intelligent, hard-working and talented academic.

However, she confessed to me that she honestly didn't think she was very good and that her appointment as Professor came about simply to boost statistics for female promotions within the university. When I asked about the invitations to write books and speak at conferences she brushed it away saying that there weren't many people working in her field so it was almost inevitable that they would have to ask her. We discussed her punishing work schedule, which she explained away as being necessary if she was simply to keep her head above water and avoid being left behind... In her opinion, she was doing alright but she wasn't as good as she ought to be and she certainly couldn't compare herself and her achievements with those of her obviously more gifted (male) colleagues.

You might think this conversation is rare, but in fact it is typical of many I've had with people in different professions who feel that they are just not good enough. And this bright, intelligent woman is not alone, which is why I have written this book.

Is this you?

You have a significant post or a role that is important or demanding yet you feel you've been lucky to get where you are today. In fact, you may believe your success is largely due to being in the right place at the right time rather than because you're talented or capable. You believe you 'somehow' managed to get the grades, even pass the exam or amazingly managed to bluff your way through the job interview. Perhaps colleagues or clients come to you for advice and you simply feel that you're 'winging it', making it up as you go along and – to your constant amazement – people seem to think you're an expert!

If you resonate with the feelings described in that last paragraph, you may well be affected by feelings of being an imposter. This feeling is more than the discomfort that comes from stepping outside your comfort zone or having to learn something new and unfamiliar. It has been described as the Imposter Phenomenon or Imposter Syndrome. You can find out more by downloading the free information sheet and questionnaire from my website at: https://MargaretCollins.com/ImposterQuestions.

Sometimes this feeling of not being good enough is entirely appropriate because we are new in post or inexperienced in our role. Maybe we're just starting out and beginning to learn. In these situations, the knowledge that we are not good enough yet is perfectly appropriate. What I want to talk about in this book is very different.

This book is for people who know they have some skills and talents, who know they have many achievements and can see ample evidence of their success yet still doubt they are really good enough. Deep down, they fear being found out as a fraud.

Although Imposter Syndrome can affect you in many situations in your life, in this book I'm going to focus on work or professional situations as that is often where the problems and stresses are most acute. If these feelings of being an imposter are familiar to you and you'd like to change them so you feel better about yourself, this book is for you. The aim is to help you recognise your imposter feelings, create a simple strategy for dealing with them and raise your confidence and self-esteem so you can experience the world as the talented individual you are, not as an imposter.

How this book is organised

This book is organised in three parts:

Part 1 explores where imposter feelings come from so you can understand that it's not just you and that you're neither alone nor some sort of freak.

Part 2 invites you to understand what these feelings mean for you and how they affect your performance and your experience of stress and anxiety.

Part 3 looks at a number of strategies you can use to build your confidence and self-esteem, challenge the way you think and discover your confidence beyond imposter syndrome.

There isn't a 'one size fits all' solution for imposter feelings as we are all different so I will share a number of practical steps you can take, all of which are based on the latest research from leading psychologists, social scientists and neuroscientists. You can then use these simple methods to retrain your thoughts, change your behaviour and set you free from your imposter habits. Find what works best for you and you will soon begin to notice the difference in the way you feel about yourself and your abilities.

Please share

If you like what you read in this book, please recommend it to anyone you believe would benefit from it by taking a minute to leave a review on the Amazon website or a comment on my Facebook page: Facebook.com/MargaretCollinsBusinessPage. I would really appreciate your support in challenging imposter syndrome and helping others to feel more confident.

Beyond
Imposter Syndrome

Introduction

Imposter what?

"EVERY TIME I WAS CALLED ON IN CLASS,
I was sure that I was about to embarrass myself. Every time I took a test, I was sure that it had gone badly. And every time I didn't embarrass myself — or even excelled — I believed that I had fooled everyone yet again. One day soon, the jig would be up ... This phenomenon of capable people being plagued by self-doubt has a name — the impostor syndrome. Both men and women are susceptible to the impostor syndrome, but women tend to experience it more intensely and be more limited by it."

- SHERYL SANDBERG

Introduction
Imposter what?

The imposter phenomenon was first revealed by Professor Pauline Clance and Dr Suzanne Imes from Georgia State University in an academic journal (Psychotherapy: Theory, Research and Practice volume 15, 1978). For their article, Clance and Imes interviewed some very talented, high-achieving women. They reported that these women felt unable to properly accept or own their professional achievements. These women (who were obviously very successful academically) felt they were frauds, that they had only 'made it' because someone had made a mistake in letting them in and that someday soon they would be found out and asked to leave their college!

The imposter phenomenon was researched more deeply over the years and gradually came to be known as Imposter Syndrome. However, I want to be clear that this is not a 'syndrome' in the medical sense. There is not something diagnosably wrong with you or that needs treatment so it can be 'put right'. Imposter Syndrome is better described as a collection of feelings or attitudes around not being good enough which can undermine your confidence in certain situations.

So, you probably will not feel like an imposter in every situation. There are likely to be many things you feel confident that you can do well and with skill. In other important situations, imposter feelings may well emerge where you are on edge, uncertain or lack confidence.

Although your levels of confidence vary in relation to different

3

activities, the more often you feel challenged in a range of different areas – or in one key area – of your life the more likely this is to affect your overall level of self-esteem. What frequently characterises people affected by Imposter Syndrome is that their peers or colleagues think they are doing a great job while they are wracked by self-doubt.

In a strange sort of way, your experience of imposter feelings is a sign that you probably are quite good at this. People with no skill nor ambition to be better don't really feel like imposters at all!

So, what situations am I thinking of here? Imposter Syndrome can affect us anywhere and in any situation. Let's take the example of the office expert. They are the 'go-to' person at work because they seem to know the ropes and people trust them – yet deep inside they feel as if they're grasping, stretching and making it up as they go along. Or maybe the example of new parents. When faced with the reality of caring for their first child, new parents often wonder "What am I doing here? I don't have a clue!!" yet they are consulted by other new parents for advice because they seem to know what they are doing.

Who is affected by Imposter Syndrome?

Initially, it was thought that Imposter Syndrome affected a relatively small proportion of high-achieving women but as more research was done, it became apparent that this phenomenon affected up to 70 per cent of both women and men at some point in their careers.

You may be affected by Imposter Syndrome if, in the face of evidence of achievement and despite repeatedly showing obvious ability:

- you feel you don't really deserve this.
- emotionally you don't 'own' your success.
- you believe if you can do it anyone can!
- you fear that one day you'll be found out.

The thing is that, even though these feelings are common, imposters feel alone and isolated, as if they are the only person in the world keeping this dark and secret fear.

In that first published paper, Clance and Imes described how feelings of being an imposter contributed to the increased levels of stress and anxiety in the women they interviewed. This is because women who revealed their imposter feelings frequently tried to hide their supposed deficiencies by consistently over-preparing for work tasks or activities because they didn't want to lose their jobs, careers or college places. This is why many imposters have impossibly high standards and feel the need to work longer and harder simply to keep up. Failing in public is just not an option for them. It also means they frequently hold back, don't stretch for opportunities or play safe because they fear they are not good enough to go for what they want.

Another observation made by Clance and Imes was that those who identified as imposters often developed good relationships with more senior or powerful colleagues. This sounds great but in fact it led to those with the syndrome believing they only kept their jobs because other people liked them or because they were being nice to them.

Imposters often undermine the value of their own work in a bid to prepare for the day they will be found out. It's almost as if imposters constantly tell others "No, it's not really that good, honestly." so that when they are discovered to be imposters they can also tell those others "See, I told you I wasn't that good!" On the surface this might look like false modesty but somehow in the mind of an imposter the ideas that they can produce good work and still not be good enough seems to sit comfortably side by side. This collection of behaviours is a real source of stress and keeps imposters playing small and staying safe rather than growing and making the contributions they are capable of. If you are personally familiar with similar feelings, then it is possible that you too are experiencing Imposter Syndrome.

Almost anyone can be affected by Imposter Syndrome, even famous celebrities. It proves that being famous and achieving great success does not prevent people from imposter feelings. When the actress Jodie Foster was interviewed for the television show '60 Minutes' she revealed how she feared she'd have to give back her Oscar after being voted best actor for her role in 'The Accused'. "I thought it was a fluke," she said in the interview. "I thought everybody would find out and they'd take the Oscar back. They'd come to my house, knocking on the door, 'Excuse me, we meant to give that to someone else. That was going to Meryl Streep.'"

What makes this even more amusing is that when Ken Burns interviewed Meryl Streep, the most frequently nominated Academy Award and Golden Globe actor in history, she revealed her own insecurities "You think, 'Why would anyone want to see me again in a movie? And I don't know how to act anyway, so why am I doing this?'"

And of course, as you read about Jodie Foster and Meryl Streep you're probably thinking something along the lines of "Yes, I can see how they might think they were imposters... and that might be nice or comforting but that's not like me because I'm a real imposter!". Imposters always feel so isolated!

Further research also shows that there are real differences in the experience of Imposter Syndrome between men and women and those who are part of a visible minority. This is because the effects of affirmative action strategies can leave the people it is designed to help wondering whether they are good enough or whether they were simply appointed to fulfil a written or unwritten quota. This doubt in turn adds to feelings of being undeserving and this reinforces feelings of being an imposter.

The good news is that no matter how you have come to your own particular version of imposterhood, you're not alone, in fact, you're in great company and there are some simple ways to reduce the frequency and intensity of these feelings.

It may be worth remembering some of the tools you need to take on this journey. Brené Brown talks about needing three things before stepping out into the wilderness:

- Courage: the willingness to tell your own story from your heart, to be yourself rather than hide behind a false identity.

- Compassion: the ability to feel pain and still move forwards rather than to hide or bury your pain under layers of tough armour.

- Connection: the profound strength that comes of being in touch with our own core values and reaching out to people who love and respect us because of our individuality and quirks, not in spite of them.

Yes, it is possible to move beyond your imposter and to be your best version of yourself.

PART 1

Sources of imposter feelings

"AUTHENTICITY IS A COLLECTION OF CHOICES that we have to make every day. It's about the choice to show up and be real. The choice to be honest. The choice to let our true selves be seen."

– BRENÉ BROWN

PART 1
Sources of imposter feelings

In this section, we are going to look at where your imposter feelings may come from and how you can recognise them.

Who experiences Imposter Syndrome?

Many studies have looked at the types of people who experience imposter feelings and compared their backgrounds and life experiences. It seems that several factors might make it more or less likely that you have these feelings. Below is a summary of the situations where people are most likely to develop Imposter Syndrome.

People who are the first or in a minority
In this instance, you may develop Imposter Syndrome because you were considered unusual by people 'at home' in your family or community.

- The first professional in your family.
- The first to go to university.
- The first to hold a particular job in your workplace.

People who are atypical in their field
For whatever reason, you are clearly different to the people around you and that contributes to the feeling that you don't belong in some way.

Funny because we are all unique

11

- A female engineer.
- A male midwife.
- A woman who has achieved success in a traditionally male industry.

People with high achieving/outstanding parents

Whether expressed or not, there is often a feeling of doubt, "Am I here because of my own achievements or because people know my family?"

- People who have to live up to the high expectations of their parents.
- People who struggle to separate their own achievements from those of their parents e.g. they may feel uncertain as to whether their achievements are theirs or due to their parents' connections.

People who feel they have to live up to the high expectations of others

One of the additional challenges here is that achieving success doesn't end this pressure. As soon as one goal is achieved another one appears and there is an expansion of expectation every time.

- People who are always under pressure to achieve.
- People who are frequently compared to the performance of siblings or other close relatives.
- People who are identified by teachers as gifted or capable of great achievements yet feel they always let people down or don't achieve their potential.

People who achieved success unusually early or easily

People may have told you that a task will be difficult so you'll need to 'knuckle down', focus and work hard. Yet you sailed across the finishing line with ease and grace. This can lead to concern that success cannot be repeated: "It was so easy the first time. Will I be able to do it again?"

- People who achieved success with apparent ease doing something regarded as challenging.
- People who achieved success when they were unusually young.
- People who achieved success early in their career.

People who work in creative activities or who work alone

Artists, writers and creatives often have no means of objectively comparing their work to an external standard so they feel insecure. Researchers and people doing PhDs may work within larger research teams but each project is unique, their own, making it difficult to compare to others. Often judgements of quality are only made when the final publication or thesis appears, which can create intense insecurity during the process of creating it.

- People who work alone – i.e. entrepreneurs.
- People who work in creative industries or professions.
- People who are in isolated or unique roles.

In looking at these "risk factors" you might find you fit a type or not. We're not looking to make you fit nor to fix anything at all, just to notice what may have contributed to your experiences.

Where do imposter feelings come from?

The origins of imposter feelings are many and complex. Research suggests that certain experiences and situations may contribute to the development of imposter feelings. Look through the following list and see whether you recognise any of the events or whether the messages seem familiar to you.

Family dynamics

- You received mixed messages about your abilities. For example, you were seen differently at home and at school.
- You were told: "Be smart – make something of yourself!" (or else!)
- You felt different, like a square peg in a round hole. You were always the odd one out e.g. the scientist in a family of musicians.
- There was a lack of praise, recognition or appreciation for your achievements: "Don't be big-headed!"
- You were the victim of family labels: e.g. "You're not the smart one."

Early messages and expectations

- You always felt you were falling short.
- You were always exceeding expectations (this can also lead to Imposter feelings).
- You did things that were totally different or completely unexpected.
- You didn't meet your own or your family's expectations for you e.g. you were supposed to:

- follow in the family footsteps.
- get married and have children.
- get a proper job.
- get a job with a typical woman's or man's role.

If you find that you are not living up to the expectations of your family or community it may contribute to you feeling like a fraud or an imposter.

> "Typically, women are expected to be better at building relationships and caring for others. They are regarded as natural supporters, not leaders. Most women are not good at maths, science, construction or engineering. They follow orders, they don't give instructions. Women are meant to be nice and of course, they are always sensitive and very emotional. By contrast, men are leaders, they are direct, they give orders and they are confident, certain and strong."

As you read that description, you may find yourself strongly disagreeing with this stereotypical view of women or men. You may not believe or agree with this stereotype but research has shown that these stereotypes still affect us, which is why we are now going to explore the field of unconscious bias.

Women and men who are successful in ways that are different to their gender stereotypes (for example, women who are leaders or men who are caring or empathetic) often experience more difficulties in life or work as they are seen as violating societal gender expectations. Some of these feelings are internalised and affect how they feel about themselves.

In many cases, bias is expressed by others around us, such as our peers and our managers. There is a large body of research that exemplifies often subtle and indirect discrimination in the workplace at many levels. These biases can also feed into feelings of insecurity and frustration. So, let's spend a little time exploring unconscious or implicit bias in more detail.

Unconscious or implicit bias

The concept of implicit or unconscious bias has been well established by a large body of research. As the name suggests, it is often unconscious, which means it's something we are unaware of but is still a significant part of our social identity. Implicit bias has two main components:

1. We tend to use social schemas (what we believe we know about categories, types, things or people) to speed up our decision-making when faced with lots of information.

2. We are more likely to respond positively to people who are 'like us' and react against people who are different to us or may not fit in.

What are social schemas and how can they be helpful or unhelpful?

Imagine that you're planning a 16th birthday party and you're wondering what food to provide or prepare. First, you think about the young people who have been invited to the party individually and you realise you don't know them very well. This means you are struggling to know what their individual likes or dislikes might be when it comes to food and drink. Then you think of the young people attending the party as a group and the lightbulb moment happens as you think "Teenagers!" You now have clearer ideas about what food and drink to provide – and how much of it!

I'd like to share an example of where such schemas can be more surprising by asking you two questions?

1. What do you imagine when you think of single parents?

2. If you wanted to create social policy or provide services to support single parents what would you think of making available?

Now I don't know what thoughts came to your mind but surveys show that when asked about single parents most people think of teenage mums, young girls who got pregnant while still young and are now dependent on their parents or the benefits system. When they think of services or support they need people tend to think of small starter homes and crèche facilities for small babies. However, the reality is that the average single mother in the UK is 38 years old and is far more likely to be a mature woman who is divorced or separated from her partner than a teenager. Such a mother is more likely to need a four-bedroom house than a starter home and after-school clubs rather than a crèche.

I remember being at the unfortunate end of such a stereotypical judgement many years ago. I was 29 years old and an enthusiastic and engaging young woman (I thought!). I had blonde hair, blue eyes and stood 5ft tall in my socks. I was also the proud owner of a small 50cc Honda moped with a top speed of 32 miles per hour.

One Sunday, I rode out into the countryside in search of lunch and found a typical British idyll: a pub beside a pond with people playing cricket on the village green. What a place to stop for lunch! I parked my moped and went into the pub to order lunch carrying my motorcycle helmet on my arm. I was most disappointed to be told, "We don't serve bikers here", as I really didn't feel that me and my tiny moped fitted the description of a "biker" at all!

When social schemas become particularly unhelpful is when you start to think of roles such as scientist, nurse, or even manager. Most people automatically think of scientists as being male and nurses as being female. Even managers are far more likely to be imagined as male than female. The idea of this doesn't help your job prospects or increase your comfort in your role if you turn out to be different to that stereotypical image. "Barrister" rarely brings up the image of a successful black woman. Expectations are also associated with things like age, race or even height and weight.

There is a double edge here:

- you may find that other people show bias against you because they don't expect someone like you to do your job.
- at the same time, you may find you feel uncertain or insecure because you notice that there aren't many people like you round here.

Implicit bias affects everyone, both men and women, in a wide range of circumstances. I'll include a selection of research references at the end of the book and, for ease of reading, simply include some major examples here.

Bias starts to affect us even when we are children. We know that boys and girls, men and women are physically different. However, research studies have shown that adults treat small children differently depending on whether they think the child is a boy or a girl because of the baby clothes worn by the child. The adult offers the child a matching 'boy's toy' or a 'girl's toy' and believes it was the child who expressed the preference. What is surprising is that the difference between toys marketed for boys and those for girls (for example toy soldiers for boys and princess dolls for girls) is more extreme today than it was in the 1970s. While there are real biological differences between boys and girls, these natural differences are exaggerated and encouraged from their earliest ages by socialisation and stereotypes as presented in marketing and advertising.

When I first read about implicit bias I admit I was sceptical and it might be that you are thinking something similar. Yes, bias exists but maybe not as much as this and not affecting as many individuals or groups. After all, I suspect you feel you're not biased and neither are your friends and colleagues... I remember feeling that too and then I read the research!

Social attitudes to boys and girls also shape behaviour. Even in childhood boys tend to play games without rigid rules or are rewarded and valued when they break the rules. For girls, 'standing out' is often not rewarded. A girl who is noisy or answers back might be told "That's not nice. Don't be bossy" while a boy might be sent outside with the comment that "Boys will be boys". These small and seemingly insignificant differences slowly accumulate until we, as individuals and as groups, expect that men are leaders or mavericks and women are natural carers and compliant. This is an example of implicit bias around gender.

Even professional musicians are not immune from unconscious bias. When auditioned for places in professional orchestras, after listening to people play, you might assume that any professional orchestra would select the best musician irrespective of their gender. It turned out that most successful applicants turned out to be male. A research study (published in 2000) revealed that when the audition was changed so that musicians played behind a screen, the number of female musicians recruited increased dramatically. This revealed an implicit bias for male musicians but it almost certainly wasn't intentional. The interviewers wanted the best players in the orchestra but their interpretation of 'best' seems to have been influenced by a deep unconscious belief that men were better musicians than women.

There are also studies which show that we assess people's career success and potential for job success by gender. A case study based on the career of a successful venture capitalist was assessed by a class of college students. Unknown to them, a single detail was changed for half the class, the gender of the person being reviewed. So half the class reviewed Heidi while the other half reviewed Howard. It seems that Howard was successful, savvy and an all round great guy. Heidi in contrast was scheming, manipulative and not a very likeable person. (See McGinn and Tempest, Harvard Business School, 2010). This piece of research illustrates that success and likeability are positively correlated for men and negatively correlated for women. It shows that in general, we don't think a nice woman can be successful in a man's world - often very challenging for professional women who feel like imposters.

When we see a man or a woman doing something different

to what is expected it causes a momentary 'stop and think' moment. When we are aware of our own potential for bias in these situations we can consciously correct our choices and behaviours. If we deny or fail to recognise our bias, it is more likely to affect our choices and to be expressed as a behaviour that results in subtle or even significant discrimination as shown in the next example.

When a CV and a speculative letter for a graduate lab manager position was circulated to a number of research active labs in North America in 2012, the exact same CV apparently described a much superior candidate who got more job offers, more offers of career support and a higher starting salary when the candidate was named John than when exactly the same credentials were attributed to Jennifer.

What is equally interesting in this case is that the results showed that the gender of the person making the job offer made no difference so it's not a case of men being biased against women. It made no difference whether the head of the lab or research team was male or female. Both men and women were affected by the unconscious bias that meant the same CV was viewed more positively if attributed to a male applicant.

As adults, we know these gender stereotypes are not true but they still affect our unconscious decisions and choices unless we make a conscious effort to eliminate bias. Pretending that bias doesn't exist and doesn't affect our behaviour has been shown to be a poor way to avoid bias and discrimination.

So, unconscious or implicit bias is real and affects both men and women but what has this got to do with Imposter Syndrome?

The unconscious knowledge we absorb from social stereotypes affects how we feel about ourselves and our roles, whether we are behaving according to our type or doing something different to what is expected of us by ourselves, our families, colleagues or society.

When we are in roles that in some way contradict this bias or expectation we are more likely to feel we shouldn't be there and that we are a fraud or an imposter, even though logically and rationally we know this is not true. It is precisely the unconscious nature of the bias that leaves us caught between what we know logically and the gut feeling that something's not right. That means we know we're not an imposter at the same time as we truly feel we're not good enough and one day someone will find out!

It's also likely that these social stereotypes are one reason why we feel that women are more likely to say they are imposters than men. The social penalties for a man who admits to feeling weakness or uncertainty are harsh and boys quickly learn to bluff or show bravado because fear isn't an acceptable emotion amongst their peers. The ability to 'wing it', improvise in the moment and look stronger than you feel is a skill that boys learn to master very quickly. So perhaps we shouldn't be surprised to learn that men who experience imposter feelings are also experts at 'bluffing it' too.

What do you remember?

Now it's time for you to reflect on your own recollections and experiences of imposter feelings. It might be that memories tumble forth or you may find you have to dig a little deeper.

Do you remember family expectations or situations that might contribute to your feelings of being an Imposter?

- Have you surprised your family or peers?

22

- Was it important to hide your talents so others wouldn't be upset?
- Was your success something of a surprise to you or those around you?
- Have you crossed stereotype boundaries or worked in an environment where you have felt different for some reason, perhaps because of your gender, race or religion?

I'm not encouraging you to fit any boxes or stereotypes, simply to take the time to explore what might be relevant to you. If you are experiencing feelings of being an imposter it can sometimes be helpful to understand where these may have come from. Remember that throughout our lives we receive many very subtle (and some not so subtle) yet extremely powerful messages that influence how we think and feel. Nobody is immune to this.

Speaking personally, I was from a working-class family with no previous evidence of academic interest or achievement. Although my parents were generally supportive and often proud, they didn't expect their daughter to be an academic. I was the first person in my street and possibly from my entire neighbourhood to go to university. It was no surprise to me to discover that I had feelings that I didn't belong.

As I look back there were specific incidents that come to mind. For example, in the summer break between me getting my BSc award and starting my PhD I revisited my secondary school and attended the school summer fête.

While I was there, I bumped into my physics teacher. I had been the only girl in his class of 10 students studying physics so I had no doubt he would remember me. He was the only teacher in the school who had a PhD himself so I expected him to be very supportive when I told him that I too was going to do a PhD. Instead he looked at me and said, "Margaret, you do know there's such a thing as too much education?". To this day I'm still not quite sure what he meant or why he said that but it did hit me hard. Many of my peers from that school were already married with young children so perhaps even to him I seemed an unlikely academic. It certainly stirred seeds of doubt for me - but it didn't stop me.

This illustrates that it's even more important to remember that feelings don't make something right or fair and feelings don't need to be expressed in behaviour. Just because we feel like an imposter doesn't mean we are an imposter. Even when we do feel like an imposter we can choose to continue making our contributions and doing our job. This is one place where mindful-awareness of our feelings can be very liberating.

It can be powerful simply to notice a feeling: "Oh yes, it's that 'I'm not good enough imposter feeling again'." You can then acknowledge it: "I know where that comes from!" so you can continue to put yourself out there: "Because people like me really do this stuff!". You acknowledge the feeling and don't let it limit your behaviour. Sometimes you need to act *before* you feel ready – and these actions will begin to change your feelings.

You have to show yourself the way.

Summary of Part 1:

- Imposter Syndrome affects the majority of men and women at some time.

- Sometimes we can see influences in our early lives that made us feel different.

- Being different in some way can lead us, or others to feel that we don't belong/fit-in.

- Being different does not limit our ability to perform or do the job well.

PART 2

Understanding
your imposter feelings

"WE HAVE TO DARE TO BE OURSELVES,
however frightening or strange that self
may prove to be."

– MAY SARTON

PART 2
Understanding your imposter feelings

This self-reflective section is for you if you want to understand and move beyond your feelings of being an imposter. If you want to change the way you feel – rather than simply have an interesting read about being an imposter – then you might find it helpful to write down the questions posed here along with your answers.

A large body of educational research shows that taking the time to write out our thoughts and ideas has a significant impact on how well we process information and learn. Writing about our thoughts and feelings also helps to reduce our experience of stress and anxiety. (If you're reading on Kindle, you can write your answers as notes in the Kindle book or you can use a reflective journal – just use whatever works best for you.)

Imposter excuses: how come real imposters have achieved so much?

People affected by Imposter Syndrome are generally held in high regard by their peers or colleagues and have achieved much in their chosen field. Their colleagues don't think of them as imposters at all.

If you feel like an Imposter, take a moment to reflect on some of the things you have done and achieved so far... This list can include documented exams, degrees and other qualifications. It's also likely to include non-academic things like being the first person in your family to work away from home, to hold a challenging job while raising a family, being the only woman in the department or the only person of colour in a white middle-class organisation. What have you achieved?

The chances are that as you reflect on this you're also thinking, "Yes, but..." and a number of excuses or qualifiers come to mind. As imposters, we are often very good at explaining away our successes but it's worth being aware that not owning our own achievements is an intrinsic part of being an imposter. If you're really struggling to see your achievements, try imagining what your best friend would say if someone asked them what you had achieved.

People experiencing Imposter Syndrome sometimes grudgingly accept that they have been successful in life or work but then they give some great long explanation or excuse for their success. "No, no", they say "it's not that I'm talented!" After all, they are imposters! If you ask them, they'll say the only reason they reached a certain goal, passed a particular exam or succeeded in getting *that* job was because:

- they were lucky.
- it was just good timing.
- they were desperate to appoint someone – anyone, even me!
- the examiner was having an off day.
- they received a lot of help.
- they just had an amazingly good interview – what a fluke!

Where's the middle ground of ego? Are people afraid to celebrate in fear of ego?

30

In fact, when it comes to explaining imposter successes, any reason will do as long as it's not "Because I deserved it". Frequently, Imposters believe their successes are due to temporary, uncontrollable, external factors like luck or the good will of others. So, take a few minutes now to write out some of your thoughts.

What are your reasons or excuses for your success (despite being an imposter)?

The real price of the beliefs that your success wasn't due to something you did is that when success arises for reasons outside of you and outside of your control you have no way of knowing if you will ever be able to repeat it. This sense of being powerless or lacking control contributes to feelings of stress, discomfort and anxiety. The natural result of this stress is a part of our brain called the limbic system becomes more active triggering the fight or flight response and physically we experience a surge in levels of the hormone cortisol. The effects of these changes takes blood flow and energy away from the more rational, thinking part of our brains. This mean that when you are called upon to make a decision or to share an opinion you are more likely to experience that blank-brain moment when everything you know seems to fade from your memory, your brain fills with fog and words get stuck in your throat. Experiencing anxiety can really rob you of access to the stuff you know you know.

Maybe the most surprising reason or excuse given by imposters to explain their success is: "I was successful, yes, but only because I worked so hard!" This statement suggests that imposters believe that real success only comes easily and without effort.

Strangely, this means that if you have to work hard you're somehow cheating the system and your achievements aren't as good or as valuable. Really? Or maybe it means that if you sometimes got it wrong (and had to practice before you became proficient) that your skill is not real or is somehow devalued.

In her book *Rising Strong*, Brené Brown reflects that there's an increasing tendency to expect things to be fun, fast and easy. If something takes long hard work it's easy to assume the result isn't worth the effort or, more importantly for imposters, that the requirement for effort means they're not as good as they should be.

In their very first research paper on the imposter phenomenon, Clance and Imes described behaviours around diligence and hard work that today we might describe as perfectionism. Would you describe yourself as being a bit of a perfectionist? The idea here is that if we, as imposters, work really, really hard and produce excellent work then just possibly people won't notice that we aren't really that good and we shouldn't be here.

Brené Brown describes this outward-looking aspect of perfectionism as "what will they think of me if they see this is the work I produce?" and identified the emotion as being closely related to shame. She defines shame as the fear that we are not worthy of love and belonging – and as we know, imposters certainly fear that they don't belong. This is one reason I explore this in more depth in my workshops. After working through the exercises, one participant completely turned around her beliefs and at the end declared, "I'm not an imposter, I now see how brave I am!"

But until imposters make this discovery they will continue to believe that hard work will hide their fraudulence. And because they are often very good at what they do, their plan works – they

Get this book.

succeed and receive the award, only to live in even greater fear of being found out next time around. The fact that they worked so hard to achieve their goal (despite not being very good!) seems to undermine the value of the achievement. Maybe one of the perverse effects of Imposter Syndrome is that being successful doesn't provide satisfactory evidence of achievement. Many people would say "See, here's the evidence that shows how good I am." but to an imposter, such evidence makes the situation even worse because they now have to explain yet another fluky success.

In her book, *Mindset: The new psychology of success*, Carol Dweck explores the value of a growth mindset – that is a mindset that views failure as a simple and necessary step on the journey towards success. In contrast, a fixed mindset says that you are either good or you're not. A fixed mindset is associated with someone showing lower levels of persistence (resulting in someone giving up more easily), and lower instances of risk-taking (playing it safe instead of going for the challenging stretch. Many people who experience Imposter Syndrome experience feelings of public failure as excruciatingly painful and will secretly work long and hard to avoid any possibility of getting it wrong.

What do you believe about ability, intelligence or success? Must it always be fun, fast and easy or is repeated failure really the best way to master a skill? Many imposters feel that success is hard-earned and that it demands persistent, painstaking work but that work needs to be conducted in secret and out of public view because to admit it wasn't easy is an unacceptable sign of weakness and of being an imposter.

So, take some time to write and reflect on this.

- How much of your achievement is down to you?
- How much of your success do you attribute to luck or other people?
- Does "hard work" make success more or less valuable?

Sure, we all need a little luck in our lives and all the hard work in the world can't guarantee success but the reality is that (on balance) the more work we do and the better prepared we are, the luckier we will get. Maybe, in this context, luck is that time when years of preparation meet an unexpected opportunity... Are you ready to admit that you put in the work to prepare even if you didn't completely control the opportunity?

Attitudes to success and failure...

Many Imposters have similar attitudes to success or to failure, both of which are often learned in childhood. Research studies have shown – and your personal reflections may agree – that during play young girls are frequently concerned that they play the game according to the rules, play tends to be co-operative rather than competitive. Breaking the rules or doing something unexpected is not valued and may be punished by exclusion - you lose your friends. The intended outcome for girls is often that everyone feels good or involved rather than one person winning at a task.

In contrast, many games played by boys are relatively unstructured and competitive. They require surprise and innovation in order to win or be successful – and winning, perhaps by any means possible – is seen as being very important.

As I noted earlier, adults respond differently to a child depending on whether they are dealing with a girl or a boy. After a failure, a girl is more likely to be cared for or protected. Her "hurt" is soothed with the unspoken message that failure hurts and is something to be avoided, secret or even something to be ashamed of. By contrast, a boy is more likely to be picked up, brushed down and thrown back in to have another go. The message is that failure is a natural part of life and is to be expected and worked through until success is achieved. The common encouragement to "Man up!" shows how nothing less is acceptable behaviour for many boys and men.

These attitudes often have long-lasting effects in our adult lives as they colour our reactions to success and failure and in part account for some of the different ways adult men and women react to imposter feelings – many women tend to be risk-averse and avoid the potential shame of public failure while men (even those experiencing imposter feelings) are more likely to engage in risky behaviour to prove they are good enough.

When men or women behave in ways that don't correspond to the expected gender-rules, there are penalties in social judgement or stigmatisation. Take a moment to reflect on your own thoughts and experiences of failure and where you believe your attitudes came from.

Are you good enough?

One consistent feeling reported by imposters is that they feel they're not good enough and certainly not as good as they should be...

Many times I've walked into a room full of my peers feeling like they are the wise adults while I felt like an inexperienced adolescent. They have earned their place or position in this group because they knew what they were doing and I still had a lot to learn. When you experience thoughts and feelings like this remember that more than 70 per cent of people experience imposter feelings so there are probably several 'imposters' already in the room!

So how do feelings of 'not being good' enough affect you?

Think of one or more significant aspects of your work or personal responsibilities and reflect on how you would complete the following sentence:

If I really was good enough for this I would...

Take as much time as you need to think of as many different ways as you can to explain what you need to do to be good enough. For example:

If I really was good enough for this:
- I could answer any question correctly and without hesitation.
- I would be confident that I knew the answer.
- I would anticipate problems before they arose.
- I wouldn't feel anxious when standing at the front of the room.
- I could argue my position confidently and quickly.

Then, thinking about your answers, see if you can summarise in two or three lines what your definition of competence would be. For example:

My definition of competence reflecting the statements above is:
- I will anticipate all problems or questions even before they arise.
- I will be able to answer every question I am asked confidently and correctly.
- I will never show or feel doubt, hesitation or anxiety in public.

Do I need to ask you whether that is a reasonable definition of being good enough?! Many imposters have incredibly high standards for their own work or contributions. For them, error is not allowed and anything other than complete mastery and unhesitating confidence is unacceptable. There's always a feeling of "I should have known that" which seems to apply disproportionately to the imposter and not to everyone else.

While it can be healthy to work at self-improvement and important to set high standards in work, it's worth remembering that for most of us, literal perfection is not the norm. So, if the desire for perfection is stopping you from making good and valuable contributions then something is out of balance.

When you think of your own personal definition of "What I need to know or to do in order to be good enough", do you use the same standards of competence to evaluate, assess or judge people around you as you do for yourself? Most imposters are their own worst critics. They will frequently remember and beat themselves up for any perceived inadequacy or error long after everyone else has completely forgotten about it.

On many occasions I've held myself back from answering a question in public because I wasn't sure I knew enough. When someone else has given an answer (and rightly received praise and recognition for their contribution), I have quietly ruminated that I knew their answer to be incomplete and reflected that my knowledge was indeed good enough. The only problem was that I had lacked the courage to share in case I was seen to be wrong in public.

It's often the case that we readily own the theory that failure is a natural part of the learning process and that at the highest levels of a fast-moving field it's not possible to know everything, but when the time comes, the thought that we might be that person who doesn't have a perfect answer causes us to freeze with pain and shame.

In these situations, our logical knowledge and our feelings are in conflict and we are using double standards. If we can begin to see the inconsistency here, then we can begin to treat ourselves and to judge ourselves just a little more kindly.

It might also be helpful to remember that other people don't pay half as much attention to us as we fear they do. The spotlight effect is a phenomenon, a trick of our minds that makes us think that other people are thinking about us – and usually in a negative way. This was described several years ago in a research study (Gilovich et al. Journal of Personality. 2000) when some students were asked to wear a T-shirt with a picture that they would have found embarrassing (actually one of the singer Barry Manilow) before walking into a room full of their peers.

Although they weren't in the room long, when asked, the students felt certain that most people had noticed their uncool attire. Of course, in reality, only a fraction (about a quarter) of

38

the people had noticed what they were wearing. This goes to show that we can feel we are in the spotlight even though most people spend more time thinking about themselves than thinking about you. In fact, they are probably worrying about what you and other people think of them rather than thinking about you.

Most of us have a natural tendency to assume that other people notice us and care enough about us to remember us — our positive contributions and particularly our mistakes. The slightly more comforting truth is that other people usually don't notice us or remember what we do. People move on to other things much more quickly than we imagine. We need to remind ourselves on a regular basis that we are not as much in the spotlight as we fear!

When we do make a mistake, we need to show ourselves some compassion — at least to the same degree that we would show compassion to a friend or colleague. Developing self-compassion can be a lifelong task for some of us and both Brené Brown and Kristin Neff have much to say on the subject. In my workshops, we take time to work through some of these reflective activities to explore how we can be both realistic and self-compassionate. As you read this book the next section will allow you to explore these too - as recovering imposters can we begin to let ourselves take risks in public, remind ourselves that we are only human and be willing to treat ourselves with the same level of compassion that we would give to a trusted friend or colleague? I'm not saying it will always be easy but we can at least begin to develop the skills!

How does your imposter help you or keep you safe?

If you are reading this book it's likely that you are feeling frustrated by your imposter feelings. Deep down, one part of you knows you are more than this and better than an imposter. Another part of you still struggles to step up as your confidence is limited by your imposter feelings.

However, even though you might be willing to admit that when you get hijacked by your imposter your behaviour isn't particularly helpful, its origins and unconscious intentions probably are meant to bring you some benefits. For example, let's say you don't volunteer opinions in meetings. The potential benefit of this behaviour is that you don't make a fool of yourself in public. Playing small or being hidden can have benefits of keeping you safe from attack or criticism! Maybe you let other people hold the floor even when you know you know more than them, but deep down you feel that's one way of being respectful to them and avoiding being seen as bigheaded.

Again, though we can probably see that this isn't logical, it can still be an important source of our feelings and a motivator for our imposter behaviour. Recognising the underlying positive intent and saying "Thank you" can be a more constructive way of exploring those feelings than simply accusing ourselves of being stupid or spineless. Take a moment now to reflect on the following question and write down your answers:

How do my imposter feelings help me or keep me safe?
Often I see answers including "Keeping me safe from criticism"

or "Giving other people a chance to shine". At a deeper level it can also be about not wanting to stand out, to be more accepted as part of the crowd, about fitting-in. In social groups these can be powerful motivators, but there are other ways to make friends, to build people up and to make valuable contributions yourself without hiding your talents.

Of course, these possible benefits of being an imposter are only one side of this coin. There are distinct disadvantages to continuing this behaviour and we will look at how we use that as a motivator later.

Before we begin though, I want you to have a final push at making the decision to change by considering the following question:

What will happen if you never change?

Take out your notebook and spend some time reflecting on the price you are paying for living with your imposter feelings:

- What will happen if I never change this pattern?
- What price am I paying for holding on to these feelings?
- What opportunities am I missing?
- What options are not available to me?

For example: If I never change it means I'll never volunteer for a challenging task in case I fail in public. If I never step up, nobody will ever give me the chance to lead a project of my own. The price I will continue to pay is feeling frustrated when other people who are not as good as me do things I want to do and that I know I could do better than them. I am missing out on the opportunity to do a good job and to stretch myself. If I don't change then I will never have the chance to be recognised and valued for my skills let alone being promoted or getting a pay rise.

In reviewing the situation, are you now ready to begin to change?

Summary of Part 2:

Imposters are often successful yet they tend to:

- attribute their success to factors beyond their control.

- be particularly self-critical.

- have very high standards for personal competence.

- see failure as a personal flaw rather than a part of the learning process.

- use their imposter to keep them safe in some way.

To move beyond our imposter feelings we need to know ourselves more honestly, to accept ourselves for who we are and be prepared to be our more authentic self when with others.

self awareness.

PART 3

Reducing imposter feelings - 10 ways to take you forward

"HOW WOULD YOUR LIFE BE DIFFERENT IF …
you approached all relationships with
authenticity and honesty? Let today be
the day … you dedicate yourself to
building relationships on the solid
foundation of truth and authenticity."

– STEVE MARABOLI

PART 3

Reducing imposter feelings - 10 ways to take you forward

The beliefs and fears that are often at the root of Imposter Syndrome were often learned when we were much younger. At the time, those feelings may have been helpful and some might still keep us safe in some circumstances but probably, as adults, we are ready to consider letting go of these feelings or changing a belief that no longer serves us. In this final section, I want to draw together some of the conclusions from the previous pages into practical strategies to allow you the space to create your own action plan for reducing your imposter feelings. There is no single right way and rarely is there an instant victory. It is possible for each of us to move beyond our imposter feelings. What matters is that you choose to change in a way that makes a difference for you. The strategies I'll offer come under the following headings:

1. Deciding to change.
2. Recognise and anticipate when your imposter appears.
3. Use your logical brain to reduce feelings of fear or anxiety.
4. Have a plan for more helpful behaviours.
5. Think more helpful thoughts.
6. Show yourself some compassion.
7. Use your posture to boost confidence and reduce stress.

8.   Decide to focus on the parts that work.
9.   Change how you feel by changing what you believe.
10. Take a test drive when it comes to trying new actions.

I've arranged these in an order that makes sense to me but you can take them as you wish, just have a look and choose the combination that works for you. All I ask is that you give something a real try... I've often been surprised at how effective some things were when I didn't think they would work at all - our unconscious mind is sometimes not as logical as we might think! So give them a go, be prepared to suspend your disbelief while you assess "Does this help?" and remember, some things do take a little practice.

A battle between the unconscious mind and the logical mind

1. Decide you want to change

So far in this book, I've shared information on possible sources of the imposter feelings. My purpose was to help you see that you don't have "something wrong with you" but that you have feelings that arise when you are unconsciously influenced by your social environments. When your adult behaviours contradict these unconscious rules, you can feel as if you don't belong. Perhaps you can also see that sometimes you are your own worst critic, you do have very high standards for your work and your contributions and that these feelings can be stressful, draining or in some way significantly unhelpful for you. So, assuming you're ready to change I will now ask you to begin making some small changes, starting with the way you think about yourself and your work.

As I know I'm speaking to someone who believes they are an imposter, I realise this might seem like a big ask. After all, one of the reasons you're reading this book in the first place is that you have a long history of being highly self-critical and not feeling good enough! "If I could change the way I think and feel I wouldn't need this book" is a likely response to my request. At this point, I simply ask you to be patient with yourself. Hold on to the fact that you truly are capable of change. I'm not asking for overnight transformations – though do feel free to surprise me any time you like!

As human beings, it is in our nature to grow and to change. At a cellular level our bodies are constantly changing. Every day we learn new things. Even the most conservative of us has the capacity to grow, to learn and to adapt. At the level of our brains and our neural pathways we are also flexible. There is a fundamental principle known as Hebb's Law that, simply put, states "Cells that fire together wire together." This succinctly describes how the physical structure of our brain changes slowly but inevitably as we learn to think new thoughts and to act in new ways.

The act of thinking stimulates the growth and development of the very nerve cells that carry messages through our brains and bodies. New connections grow and are made as the nerve impulse travels along the neuronal cell extensions. The more we think the same thought or act in the same way the more those cells adapt to make carrying that particular message easier and more efficient. That's why new habits are difficult to develop at first – because we are building new neuronal cell pathways for that message to travel on. Imagine finding a simple trodden-down track through an overgrown expanse of grassland. If you choose to widen it and make it more permanent, you have to deliberately use the path over and over again until it gets wider and better defined. Eventually you might decide to make the surface of the path firm and flat, so it's even more hard-wearing. You could then maybe lay the foundations for a road, or even a dual carriageway or motorway...

You use the same process, figuratively speaking, to build new ways of thinking and behaving. As the cells that carry your new thoughts grow stronger and make more connections they become strengthened until they become the most frequently-used neural pathways. Once we commit to thinking new thoughts then repeating those thoughts or actions we strengthen the pathways and make the new thought feel more natural. Similarly, pathways that are used less – as we stop doing or thinking things that are unhelpful – get pruned and allowed to weaken until they wither, fall into disrepair and are eventually abandoned.

So, even though you might feel a little sceptical about learning to move beyond your imposter feelings, I want you to know that you too can change. You can make the decision to change as you choose to build thoughts and habits that are more helpful in overcoming your imposter feelings.

The next step is to recognise the early signs.

2. Recognise and anticipate when your imposter appears

If you want to change it is helpful to anticipate and prepare for those situations when our imposter feelings appear so we have our solutions ready. The situations or scenarios that trigger our experiences of the Impostor Syndrome are often very predictable. They may include:

- When in interviews or being tested.
- When being asked a question in front of a crowd or in a meeting.
- When delivering a presentation.
- When challenged, for example "What do you mean by...?"
- When it is necessary to argue your case to convince people.
- When negotiation is required.
- When more senior managers are asking you questions.
- When you feel you're not prepared.

When you know you are likely to walk into a situation that is likely to trigger you, don't let anxiety take you by surprise or take over. Learn to recognise the physical feelings - the rising heart rate, the feeling of panic, the warmth as your face blushes - learn to feel and to know whatever these early signs are for you personally. Not only is this going to be your greatest "early warning system" but it opens a powerful toolkit to interrupt your Imposter behaviours that we will explore in more detail in the next section.

We need to understand that as adults we can have a choice - we can act on our feelings or not. Maybe up until now our behaviour has automatically followed our feelings - for some of us the experience of imposter feelings triggers withdrawal, for others maybe it sparks bluster or confrontation. What matters here is that if we recognise the feelings we can then create space to make a decision about the behaviour or actions that we want to follow through with.

3. Use your thinking brain to reduce feelings of fear or anxiety

You can reduce the intensity and the impact of your imposter feelings by anticipating, recognising and naming them. This simple strategy works on several levels.

The act of analysing the situation, anticipating the problem and naming the symptoms or emotions is something that uses the thinking part of our brains, the prefrontal cortex. Matt Lieberman is an American researcher who has investigated this mechanism where naming difficult emotions reduces their intensity ('Putting Feelings Into Words', Psychological Science 2007). The very act of thinking requires we use energy and blood flows to the parts of the brain that need this energy. This also tends to move energy from and reduce blood flow to the limbic areas of the brain that are central to our instinctive emotional responses. It's almost as if these two areas of our brain responsible for our experience of strong negative emotion and the areas responsible for logical thought are at either end of a see-saw. When one is up, the other is likely to be down.

So, when you recognise that you are going into a situation where your imposter feelings are likely to be triggered, be prepared to activate your rational thought processes. Recognise the onset of physical symptoms, notice and name them. Although it might sound counter-intuitive it can be helpful to say to yourself "Yes, here we go again. My pulse is racing, I am feeling slightly panicky. My imposter is trying to take over again." This process of logical analysis or description of the situation means you are actively choosing to engage the thinking process which takes energy away from the emotional impact of your imposter feelings. This very simple strategy can be surprisingly effective at reducing the intensity of your imposter feelings. Note that I said 'reducing' not eliminating.

You can continue to support your desired behaviours with a plan for what to do next - your anticipated behaviour... The important thing to realise here is that you don't need your imposter feelings to go or to disappear before you start behaving differently. In fact, the same imposter feelings act as the reminder to behave differently.

4. Have a plan for more helpful behaviours

Implementation intentions in anticipation of imposter feelings or reframing are two great ways to stay on track when you fear you might be hijacked by your emotions.

For example, when I am working with clients to develop their presentation skills, they often report that they feel very anxious just at the thought of giving a presentation. Fortunately, these situations are often very predictable – we schedule most of our presentations for a specific time and date – and the work we do together preparing for that situation goes a long way to reducing the anxiety they feel. We can't always eliminate the feelings but we can create a better explanation for them.

Reframing is a fancy term for creating that better explanation for those same feelings, for example, "Yes, my pulse is racing and yes, I am breathing more quickly, but perhaps this is simply my body preparing me for an exciting challenge. I know I'm going to need more breath and more energy and here it comes! Yes, the feelings are real but they are happening in order to help me complete this task.". These reframing strategies really can change the way we think of the situation so that giving a presentation becomes a rewarding activity though be aware that you need to find a form of words or an explanation that you yourself find satisfactory. You may find someone else's explanation isn't as effective for you.

You can also remind yourself that this is nothing new and nothing unusual and you have a constructive plan for what to do next. "I recognise the start of those imposter feelings. Nothing new there but this time I'm not going to let them stop me. I'm going to be brave and ask that question anyway." These imposter feelings are not going to hijack you this time. While it might not be possible to simply switch off imposter feelings, it is possible to work a different plan.

An implementation intention can also be used to keep you on track when you are faced with a challenging situation; instead of freezing, anticipate your feelings, recognise and describe the way you feel and be prepared to fill in the blanks using a statement of anticipation.

"I'm going into a meeting with _____ and it's likely that I will feel_____ so what I'm going to do is _____."

One of my statements might look something like this: "I'm going to walk into a meeting with John (my un-favourite know-it-all) and it's likely that I will feel anxious, insecure and inadequate. If I feel challenged my pulse will race, my face will begin to flush and I'll begin to feel shut down so what I'm going to do if John challenges me is I'll take a deep breath and say "That's interesting. The research I've done suggests that my proposal will work so I propose we continue to see how it goes.".

Then when I meet with John, I'm ready. The encounter is likely to trigger my imposter feelings and I will then mentally name them. "It's happening again, the anxiety, the racing pulse, the warmth... this is simply my imposter appearing. (Deep breath) 'That's interesting John. I hear what you say though I suggest we continue as planned to see how it goes.'"

What is your statement of anticipation?

"When I _____ and it's likely that I will feel _____ so what I'm going to do is _____ ".

Many people find these reflections and adjustments to their thinking patterns make a profound difference but it might not be a magic wand. It took me a long time to work through my imposter feelings. What helped me was both the desire to change and the understanding that I could feel one thing and do something different. I could feel like running and hiding yet I could stand my ground and contribute. Certainly, my first attempts were imperfect and inelegant but it was part of a process.

The process of recognising your imposter by taking the attitude: "Hello Imposter. I see you but I'm going to do this anyway" is just one way you can begin to make decisions that are not completely limited by your emotions. But if we are going to be able to anticipate situations where our imposter feelings are triggered we need to understand what is special about those situations.

5. Thinking more helpful thoughts

When we find ourselves in situations that trigger our imposter feelings we feel as if *these situations* trigger particular emotions, feelings or behaviours. We then try to avoid the situation. While this isn't surprising, our assessment that it is the situation that causes us distress is not necessarily either accurate or helpful.

Consider people who have an intense fear of heights or snakes. They will often tell you that even thinking about the situation is enough to bring on an intense feeling of fear or dread. This experience of the feeling in the absence of the physical source should tell you something important. What causes the emotion isn't simply the object or situation but *our thoughts about that object or situation*. What has power over us is not the object or situation, it is our own thoughts.

The obvious solution would seem to be to just not have the thoughts. However, research has shown that trying to suppress our negative thoughts isn't an effective coping strategy. If you're phobic about spiders, "Don't think about spiders!" just isn't helpful advice. Trying to ignore it can make the negative experience even more intense. So, we need to find another way to change these troubling thoughts that can trigger our fears. One way is to look at the beliefs underlying our troublesome thoughts while another is to replace our fears with more helpful thoughts.

Choosing more helpful beliefs

Many of our thoughts are triggered by or are based upon our beliefs, in particular, what we believe to be true in a specific situation. If you are afraid of spiders this fear might be for many possible reasons; perhaps you simply don't like the look of them or the way they move, or maybe you believe they are dangerous. Depending on your geographic location the belief that spiders are dangerous may have a greater or lesser basis in fact. To my knowledge none of my British friends has ever been confronted with a poisonous spider here in the UK but that fact doesn't prevent some of them from holding the belief that spiders could be dangerous or stop them feeling totally terrified of all spiders that cross their path. The negative belief formed around a grain of truth (that some spiders in some places are poisonous) has expanded to form a generalisation that is extremely unhelpful.

In the context of the Imposter Syndrome, our negative thoughts and beliefs might simply reflect what we think and believe about the need to be an expert, what our real abilities are, what we believe we deserve, our potential to achieve, and much more... It is likely that each of us has slightly different thoughts and beliefs so those reasons are likely to reflect our beliefs about what it means to be less than perfect. That means the thought or belief of 'not being good enough' becomes associated with some significant and seriously negative conse-quences - I'll be rejected, lose respect, lose my job.

These beliefs and thoughts around not being good enough were often formed or learned when we were very young. It's possible that they reflect our experience of a very specific event that had some validity for us at the time but that is no longer true or relevant to us now. If we reflect on the beliefs underlying

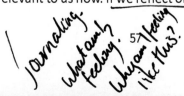

our imposter feelings we are likely to discover beliefs or feelings that are incomplete, inaccurate, even illogical, but because they are so deep we are often unconscious of them. So, if we want to change our unhelpful beliefs we need to become more conscious of them first.

Ask yourself this question: In the situations where your Imposter feelings are triggered, what is the belief that is holding you back, what is it you most fear? Your answer might look something like this:

- I don't volunteer because I'm afraid I'm not good enough and I'll fail in public.
- I don't offer opinions because I fear I don't know enough and I'll look stupid.
- If I offer an opinion and end up looking stupid nobody will ever trust or respect me again. I couldn't live with the shame and nobody would work with me again!
- I can't take the risk that I'll show myself up so I've got to be perfect all the time.

What does your version of your fear or your unhelpful belief look like?

As you reflect on or examine your belief, what do you notice? Does it seem over-generalised, limited, inaccurate, illogical or extreme? If you were brave enough to share this thought with your best friend what do you think their reaction would be?

I know, as an imposter, it is so easy to continue to doubt yourself and be critical – yet part of the strategy for moving beyond these feelings means accepting the possibility that someone else, particularly someone whose judgement we respect or trust, can give us more accurate feedback than we give ourselves. Is there any possibility that you could accept that you're being overly tough on yourself? If you're willing to believe that your fears and self-critical thoughts might be harsh or inaccurate then you are in a good position to move on to the next section though I know you might still have some doubts.

As you begin the challenge of overcoming your imposter feelings, it is helpful to decide to try new thoughts and to take new action even though you don't feel like it. At first thinking new thoughts is likely to feel unnatural, artificial and even awkward. You might feel that you're not very good at it at first but that's okay as that's what learning something new is like. Remind yourself that learning something new and being a beginner often feels uncomfortable, even though we know it's just a phase that we pass through.

If you were to imagine yourself at the start of a journey, taking one small step at a time to get beyond your imposter feelings, what positive thoughts do you think it would be helpful to think? If this seems like a strange question you might find it helpful to imagine that you are writing a novel about someone who is learning to think and act in new ways. If they were moving from imposter-bound to imposter-free what changes might they notice in the ways they think?

The exact thoughts you choose will very much depend on the situations you find challenging. Some possible helpful thoughts could include:

- Yes, I feel like a fraud but I know I'm not alone, it's a common feeling.
- It's not just me – it's uncomfortable but it's normal and I can work through it.

- Feeling like an imposter isn't the same as being an imposter.
- Many people who don't feel good enough are in fact very gifted and talented.
- It's painful to not know but asking that question is the quickest way to find out more.
- It's possible that I am judging myself harshly so what evidence am I using for this?
- How can I start to take credit for my own efforts rather than attributing success to luck?

The truth is that you need to discover thoughts that are helpful for you. They are likely to be very personal and individual to you – and it doesn't matter if those thoughts aren't necessarily logical. They just need to be helpful so that they allow you a little more freedom and flexibility in your responses and behaviour.

I used similar strategies when I decided that I was going to make more contributions in meetings, both volunteering information and answering questions. At first it felt very scary, my pulse would race, I was sure my face was red (though it wasn't) and I felt certain that everyone was watching, listening and judging me. I realised that I found it helped to make my contributions earlier in the meeting rather than later. The longer I waited to say something, the more excuses I found to back out of the challenge. As I became more accustomed to hearing my own voice, as my colleagues became more used to me making contributions, the easier it felt and the more my anxiety diminished.

What thoughts would help you to become braver or less critical?

6. Show yourself some compassion

Because things may not come easily at first (you probably have a lifetime of imposter habits to unlearn), I'm going to ask you to show yourself some compassion when you feel you still don't make the grade. If you're an exceptionally good imposter the chances are that you're not very good at showing yourself compassion so perhaps we need to look in more detail at what it means. According to Kristin Neff, a world-leading researcher in this area, self-compassion has three components:

- Self-kindness (being warm and understanding to yourself even when you feel inadequate rather than beating yourself up. Treating yourself as kindly as you would a friend in the same situation).
- Common humanity (these feelings of inadequacy are not unique to you; many, many people do feel this way, too. No matter how isolated you feel, remember that over 70 per cent of people report that they experience feeling like an imposter).
- Mindful awareness (simply noticing your feelings rather than being swept away by them or over-identifying with them. Mindful awareness allows us to realise that no matter how intense our feeling, if we let them go they will pass.)

When you have set your intention to overcome your imposter a number of things could happen. You might go from strength to strength or improvements might be slow: two steps forward and one step back. So how can you show yourself some compassion even if you feel success isn't coming as quickly or as smoothly as you would like? Again, it very much depends on the situations you face.

For example, you might decide that you are going to change your behaviour by making a positive contribution at meetings. You decide to make a comment or give an answer to a question. But then lose courage and end up staying silent. Rather than beating yourself up for not trying, show yourself some self-compassion.

- Acknowledge that after a lifetime of taking the safer imposter-driven route it's only natural that the new ways of thinking and behaving will take time to put into action.
- You are not the first, last nor only person to back down due to the fear of possibly doing something you feel is scary in public.
- Although you feel disappointed with yourself, simply notice how that feels. Decide that it will feel so much better when you find the courage to contribute. There will be another opportunity to practice soon. Until then, let the feelings go and move on.

What does it mean for you to show yourself some compassion?

7. Use your body to boost confidence and reduce stress

You are probably all familiar with the question, "Which came first, the chicken or the egg?" This age-old conundrum is now matched by the question "Which came first, the feeling or the action?" There is a large body of observational and experimental evidence that shows there is a link between how we feel with how we act. In the context of moving beyond the imposter syndrome, the feelings we want to encourage are positive feelings of confidence, the feeling that we are good enough.

The thing about feeling like an imposter is that we have very narrow criteria by which we judge ourselves to be 'good enough' and our standards are extremely high so those external measures never or rarely trigger feelings of being good enough. As a result, people who experience imposter feelings often experience stress and anxiety in situations where other people might feel confident.

So how can we boost our feelings of confidence – and will this reduce our experience of stress? The research shows that there are many ways we can use our body to create feelings of confidence and reduce our feelings of stress.

The simplest option is to just breathe: You don't need to make a big fuss about this or become some sort of breathing fanatic. Simply slow down your breathing for a minute and you'll probably notice big changes. When you breathe slowly and deeply you will experience a greater sense of calm as deep breathing stimulates an innate relaxation response. To do this, breathe in to the count of four, hold briefly at the top of your breath before breathing out to the count of four (4 x 4), pause and repeat. This slow, rhythmic breathing will stimulate a response from your parasympathetic nervous system called the 'rest and digest' response. It is the opposite of the 'fight and flight' response induced when you are anxious or stressed. It is the breathing out part of this process that has the greatest physiological effect so once you are comfortable with it you can reach an even deeper level of relaxation by breathing out slightly more slowly.

If you simply want to control your imposter feelings by avoiding a stress response then the 4 x 4 breathing pattern is probably all you need to start. Best of all, this can be done discretely in just about any situation you encounter.

Adopt a confident body posture: When people feel confident, you can usually see it in their body language because they tend to hold themselves slightly differently. Standing or sitting, they let go of any tension, their muscles relax slightly and they take up slightly more space because they spread out a little (imagine opening up slightly rather than sprawling). As they adopt this open body posture they will usually hold their heads up, they may make eye contact and even let a slight smile break across their face – and by this I don't mean you see a demonic stare and a great big grin! If you adopt a similarly positive posture, you'll begin to feel similar feelings of confidence.

There is a significant amount of research evidence that shows adopting a more relaxed and open physical posture can lead us to feel more confident. The research evidence suggests that the confident feelings come later as a consequence of the change in physical posture.

Amy Cuddy in her TED.com talk describes this process as 'Fake it 'til you become it'. She compares the different effects on how we feel when we adopt open/powerful or closed/powerless body postures. Specifically, she shows how adopting strong, open body postures or what she calls "power poses", such as a 'star pose' or a 'Wonder Woman pose' (with legs hip width apart and hands confidently planted on your hips), for just two minutes can cause significant changes in the levels of two hormones. In these circumstances, levels of testosterone (the dominance hormone) rise and levels of cortisol (a stress hormone) fall.

The result of these changes in posture is a feeling of greater confidence and an experience of less stress. So, even though we might start out feeling as if we lack confidence or courage, if we 'act as if' we are confident, even for two minutes, the hormones in our bodies will change to make that feeling become part of our real experience.

One word of advice though: if you want to use the full Wonder Woman power pose to boost your confidence you might want to do that in private. The positive effects will last a while so you can top them up by adopting an open but slightly less powerful posture in public.

So, breathing slowly and adopting an open body posture are two simple strategies that can reduce your physical and physiological experiences of stress and anxiety.

8. Focus on the parts that work

Another strategy you can use to reduce imposter feelings is to focus on positive aspects of your work rather than obsessing about how you are feeling. For many of us, the feeling of being an imposter is accompanied by the feeling that everybody is watching us as we are not being good enough. This is another example of the spotlight effect that we discussed earlier. We feel as if everybody is watching and that they remember every weakness or flaw. The truth is rather more mundane. Research confirms that we are not the centre of other peoples' universes, in fact most of the time they are not paying us that much attention, we just think (or fear) they are.

The latest research in neuroscience shows that our brains are designed to think about ourselves. When we are not actively focussed on a task – in the spaces between 'doing stuff' – we activate areas of our brain known as 'the default network'. It's the bit of our brains we use when we are not doing something specific.

So, what does this default network do? When you ask people what they are thinking about when they are not doing anything most will say they are thinking about themselves, often in social situations. We frequently either re-run things that have happened or anticipate things that we believe are going to happen.

One of most consistent features of this default network activation is that we frequently focus on what isn't going well or what isn't working. We evaluate ourselves negatively. Matthew Lieberman is a leading researcher in the area of neuroscience related to social interactions. Lieberman suggests that this function of the default network is vitally important for us. In an evolutionary sense, human beings are dependent upon their social groups for survival. In early human societies, a person couldn't survive alone. Therefore, it is entirely appropriate that our brain reflects on how we interact with others, anticipates what could go wrong and tries to figure out how to make it better.

So, although it might sound strange, this tendency to be self-focussed and to judge ourselves badly is a normal part of what our brain does when it doesn't have something specific to do. The thing is, while this was an important function many thousands of years ago, it can be quite unhelpful at times today. That means we need to use our logical minds to modify these spontaneous thought patterns. When it comes to moving beyond imposter feelings, deciding to focus on specific positive aspects of a task in hand is one of the ways of doing this.

Given that you are probably very used to thinking imposter-type thoughts this decision to choose to focus on positive aspects of a task you are actively engaged in might not feel natural at first. That doesn't mean it isn't a good strategy, though. Simply that it's a new way of thinking. Remember, you need to grow those new neural pathways! — WINS CHANNEL

So, choose to focus on the process, the bits of what you are doing that work or that could work. If you are trying to improve something, make your critical reflections constructive. It's almost inevitable that you will at some time slip into your more habitual negative thoughts, you'll notice what is going wrong and you'll decide this confirms that you are indeed an imposter. At this point it's important to remind yourself that your focus has slipped. This is the moment that you need to decide to refocus on something positive. You don't need to feel guilty, beat yourself up or wallow in your failure. Now is the time to use that third vital aspect of self-compassion, mindful-awareness, and remember that you need to notice your thoughts and feelings but not over-identify with them. Recognise that you're not doing what you want and decide to focus on the positive again. You might even allow yourself the luxury of collecting and recording your positive results, the messages of thanks and the positive feedback you receive so you can remind yourself of them when your doubts kick-in.

Susan Jeffers wrote a great book called *Feel The Fear And Do It Anyway*. The title clarifies the message in the book: namely that courageous action happens while we are still feeling fearful. This is a reminder that we need to be familiar with feeling that fear and doing it anyway. Our feelings can be different to our chosen actions. This might take time to assimilate but it's a habit that can be very successfully learned.

9. Changing how we feel by changing what we believe

If our imposter feelings really arise from the belief that we are not good enough, how can we begin to change that belief? We often develop new beliefs when we discover new evidence and information or when we learn something we didn't know before. Sometimes we already hold several different beliefs at the same time.

As imposters, we are likely to hold several beliefs (often conflicting) related to our competence or being good enough. We can of course look for external evidence of our competence but, as imposters we know we will probably find numerous reasons to doubt or disbelieve that evidence.

It is possible to mitigate this by being prepared to have faith in the opinions of people we trust and respect when they tell us that we are performing well. Reminding yourself that you respect their opinions might help you to believe they are not just being kind. Reading the positive feedback you collected might also help. But again, because we are committed imposters, this isn't likely to create the change we want so that means we also need to look at changing the beliefs that are holding us back.

If we return to those beliefs about spiders that are so problematic to some people, we can see that the people with the most severe phobias might believe that all spiders are dangerous and aggressive and can be found everywhere. You can probably understand that if you really believed this then your behaviour might be severely impacted.

If you want to learn to wriggle free from unhelpful beliefs it is often worth looking for beliefs that will be more helpful in the circumstances. That means selecting a belief that is more limited and specific rather than global and all-encompassing. This isn't simply an exercise in wishful thinking or making things up, it's about looking to create beliefs that allow you to expand your comfort zone.

So, it is possible that your fear of spiders could be based on a slightly narrower belief that *some* spiders are poisonous and they *could* be found in close proximity. In this situation, notice that this slight shift in belief has now opened up the possibility of holding the belief that there are *no* poisonous spiders *close* to us right now.

So, back to your imposter... Even as a committed imposter it is unlikely that you *always* believe you are not good enough at *anything*. There must be times when you know you are competent. You can butter bread, you can search the internet, and you can drive a car. Maybe you can even believe that you don't have to be the best in the world to be good enough to do your job.

Is there even a possibility that when you think of the situation where your imposter most frequently appears, you recognise you have some level of talent or skill. Can you accept that if you were completely and totally unsuited for your job it is unlikely that you would have been appointed to it or kept in post? As you think of your day to day performance can you see that you demonstrate some degree of skill or achievement? Can you grudgingly admit that you can believe that you can do *this* if not *that*, you know *this much*, even if that's not perfect or enough for your standards?

As you begin to think about selecting a new positive belief, make it empowering, make it positive and make it helpful. Maybe something like:

- I am intelligent and capable of doing my job to the required standard.
- I am a hard-working and valuable colleague with the right to make occasional mistakes.
- I can contribute a lot while still growing and learning more.
- I have the right to be less than perfect while becoming better at my job.
- Good enough and done is better than perfect and not finished on time!

Once you begin to think about possible positive and helpful beliefs remember that there is no 'one right way' of doing this. It might take some time and a few creative diversions before you find a belief that is both positive and helpful, and that sits comfortably with you. The reason this is so important is because our thoughts, beliefs and actions are all connected so they all influence how we feel. That means we can change how we feel by starting to change the way we think and what we do – in fact, this approach is the foundation of various forms of cognitive behavioural therapies, so it definitely works.

In the same way that Amy Cuddy has shown that the way we behave can affect the way we feel (remember the 'fake it 'til you become it' power poses?) there is also evidence that the way we think affects the way we feel. When it comes to moving beyond our imposter feelings it is important to use this combination of tools – the choices we make about the actions we take, the thoughts we choose to think, the beliefs we decide to hold – to make many smaller changes that eventually deliver big improvements in the way we feel about ourselves.

10. Take a test drive

Trying out your new beliefs will probably feel a little strange at first. Your old beliefs will feel like a comfortable pair of shoes while your new beliefs might feel tight and awkward. Accept that your new thinking and behaviour will feel strange and that this is a normal part of learning something new.

So, let's see how we can break in your new habits. New skills and attitudes will grow and develop as they are used more and more. Can you think of some meetings you are going to where you could make a commitment to speak up, step out or stretch out of your comfort zone? Ideally, think of some situations where you can begin to safely test your new beliefs without the risk of getting blisters or scars. Be willing to feel a little vulnerable.

Brené Brown has written and researched the links between

courage and vulnerability. She concludes that our willingness to make ourselves vulnerable is the greatest measure of human courage as our natural instincts would have us either retreat and hide or put on so much armour that we are completely invisible beneath it. She writes, "If we want to be courageous and we want to be in the arena, we're going to get our butts kicked. There is no option. If you want to be brave and show up in your life, you're going to fail. You're going to stumble. You're going to fall. It's part of showing up."

As a recovering imposter, I read that and to be honest I was disappointed. You mean there is no magic way to avoid the pain and risk that comes from possible failure?!! What I discovered – and what I now share in my workshops – is that this truth tells us about the essence of being fully human and that it is accepting our own vulnerability that is the key to being quietly confident in our lives.

The truth is that Brené Brown, Carol Dweck and Susan Jeffers are all sharing aspects of the same wise message: it is impossible to live a meaningful or rewarding life and at the same time avoid any possibility of vulnerability or failure. If you want to live, if you want to contribute or to make a difference you will always run the risk of failure or rejection. There are no magic wands to take away these most vital aspects of the human experience.

However, we can learn to prepare for these situations. We can learn to appreciate ourselves and our contributions. We can learn to recognise when our Imposter feelings are likely to rise up and get in our way, encouraging us to withdraw, to hide or to play it safe by staying small.

So now it is time to go and put some of this into practice. Remember, it's okay to play! So find a meeting and decide to make a contribution. At first it can be as prepared as you need it to be. There will still be that time where you need to positively "jump", to add your voice, your comment to the mix. And yes, your heart will beat and your pulse will race and you might feel like an imposter but keep on and do it. Notice afterwards that it didn't kill you!

It's also possible that things won't go perfectly at first and that's fine, too... it's a different way of learning and failure gives you feedback – ask yourself (constructively and compassionately) what can you do differently next time? A different place, differ-ent contribution, less preparation, more spontaneity - stretch your comfort zone but slowly. Choose a safe place to have a practice as you learn these new skills.

Your personal action plan

One of my intentions in writing this book is to show you that experiencing imposter feelings isn't freaky; in fact, it's pretty normal. That doesn't mean it's not significant. I know it can cause stress and anxiety and it can stop good people making contribu-tions in situations where their skill and expertise is desperately needed.

I hope you have found it helpful to discover how social expec-tations and unconscious bias can contribute to feelings of not fitting in or feeling like a fraud. Again, the more you understand these influences the more likely you are to give yourself a better chance of handling them well.

Sometimes we need to take small steps to be kinder to our-selves, to judge ourselves less harshly and to show ourselves some compassion. We need to accept that our perception of being viewed in a critical way by others when we are in the spotlight is a cruel trick of our psyche and that it's just the natural way that our brains work. As a recovering imposter, I hope that you will want to explore a number of new beliefs, attitudes and skills. For example, it might be that you want to believe:

- It's okay to be good enough.
- Perfection isn't an absolute requirement.
- Failure is a part of the learning process.
- You're good enough and can get even better.
- *Making* a mistake isn't the same as *being* a mistake.
- There are always things we don't know yet, and that's fine.
- You can learn and improve while working on the job.

What matters is that you choose to change in way that makes a difference for you. Which of the '10 ways to take you forward' is most interesting to you? It might be one thing, it may be a combination of things but with patience and persistence it is possible to significantly change the way you feel. I don't know if we ever completely "kill-off" our imposters. I do know it is possible to move beyond our imposter feelings and act more confidently in our lives and in our work!

What does your Imposter Action Plan look like?

There are many suggestions for moving beyond Imposter Syndrome covered in this book, but where will you start? The 'best place' might be different for each of us, depending on our particular imposter feelings and challenging situations. What matters is that we do start, that we implement some of these strategies and begin to change. To help you to decide I've created an Imposter Action Plan Template. Do visit my website and **download your free copy of the Imposter Action Plan Template** and create your own plan to defeat your imposter feelings.

Summary of Part 3:

- There are many (at least ten) different ways to overcome imposter feelings.
- Some benefits might grow slowly as we expand our comfort zones and develop new habits or new ways of thinking - but grow they will if we keep doing it.
- You can have a plan, you can change your thoughts or beliefs and you can use your body to help you feel more confident.
- Be kind to yourself as you grow. Patience and persistence will win the day.
- Look for opportunities to put your plans into action, focus on what works for you.

A True Story

"I WANT TO BE IN THE ARENA.

I want to be brave with my life. And when we make the choice to dare greatly, we sign up to get our asses kicked. We can choose courage or we can choose comfort, but we can't have both. Not at the same time. Vulnerability is not winning or losing; it's having the courage to show up and be seen when we have no control over the outcome. Vulnerability is not weakness; it's our greatest measure of courage."

– BRENÉ BROWN

A True Story

Many years ago, I accepted a new job that was very different to anything I thought I would do. I moved to a new place with new people and in a new subject area that was different to anything I'd ever done before – but I knew it was a great opportunity for me. Of course, my imposter feelings screamed loud and long and I believed they were right.

After a few months in my new post, I realised that I was behaving in some very uncharacteristic ways. I was even volunteering to do work that I knew I didn't know how to do and then working very hard to catch up, find out more and learn the ropes. As a result, I was feeling stressed, anxious and exhausted.

A little reflection showed me that many of my greatest difficulties arose from conversations with my new Head of Department (let's call him Barry), a large and imposing man who was an internationally renowned expert in his field. When he was around, I found myself agreeing to requests and even volunteering for assignments that were way above and beyond anything a new member of staff needed to do to prove herself!

I realised many of these fateful conversations took place when Barry came into my small office unannounced and had conversations while standing right next to me as I sat at my desk. He was definitely in my personal space and being so tall, he towered over me. I felt like a small child and experienced significant psychological pressure to do as I was asked. After all, I reasoned, 'Barry the Expert' must know best what was 'normal' for a new member of staff and what I could reasonably be expected to do.

Yes, I was young, I was inexperienced and I was trying to prove myself. I was making every attempt to fit in, be helpful and get on... yet I knew something wasn't right. I decided to make some small changes and began to work on some of my beliefs and self-talk in the following way: "Barry might well be an expert in his field but he isn't a specialist in mine. He might know lots of things that I don't know but he doesn't necessarily know what is best for me or what I am capable of doing. And yes, I could say no as a respectful colleague or even volunteer for things I am already good at but..." You get the idea.

After this, I placed a spare seat against the office wall, opposite my desk. Then, as soon as I heard the sound of Barry's hand on the handle of my office door I stood up from my desk, opened the door from the inside and spreading my arms wide (my left hand on the door handle, my right arm pointing to the empty chair), I welcomed Barry into my office and asked him to sit down. In fact, I didn't let go of the door handle or put my arms down until he had effectively been funnelled into the waiting, empty seat.

At that point I informally perched myself on my desk, leaning back so I was half-standing and half sitting. That meant my eye level was higher than his. Strangely, from that moment on our conversations became very different and, interestingly, there were far fewer unannounced visits. My workload stabilised, my self-confidence grew and I began to carve my own niche and develop my role in the department.

None of the changes I made were revolutionary. At first, I didn't totally believe my new thoughts; I just acted as if I did. It certainly wasn't an instant miracle but it took less time than I thought it would to feel comfortable with these new ways of thinking and being. I had created the space for a more authentic version of me to emerge and blossom.

References

Articles and studies

Identification of imposter phenomenon: Professor Pauline Clance and Dr Suzanne Imes, 'Psychotherapy: Theory, Research and Practice', volume 15, 1978.

Article about differing treatment of children depending on sex publishing by scicurious:
http://scicurious.scientopia.org/2011/03/09/baby-boy-baby-girl-baby-x/

Gendered toys: The experiment: https://youtu.be/nWu44AqF0il

Elizabeth Sweet article about gender divisions in children's toys in 'The Atlantic':
http://www.theatlantic.com/business/archive/2014/12/toys-are-more-divided-by-gender-now-than-they-were-50-years-ago/383556/).

Blind auditions experiment: C. Goldin, and C. Rouse (2000) 'Orchestrating impartiality: the impact of "blind" auditions on female musicians', American Economic Review, Vol. 90, No. 4, pp. 715-741.

Heidi Roizin case study: McGinn and Tempest, Harvard Business School, 2010.

Gender bias research study: Moss-Racusin et al, 'Science faculty's subtle gender biases favor male students', Proceedings of the National Academy of Sciences, 2012.

Article about the motherhood penalty: Shelly Correll et al (2007), American Journal of Sociology, vol. 112

Amy Cuddy, Your Body Language Shapes Who You Are, (2012), ('Fake it 'til you become it' theory): TED.com

Books

Rising Strong, Brené Brown, Vermilion, 2015

Mindset: The new psychology of success, Carol Dweck, Ballantine Books, 2006

Feel The Fear And Do It Anyway, Susan Jeffers, Vermilion, 2007

Would you like to work with me?

This book contains all the information you need to start to feel more confident and less of an imposter. It can help you move beyond your imposter feelings and start to believe that you are more than good enough to meet any of the challenges ahead of you.

You might be ready to do more work or you might want a little company along the way, in which case I'd really like to hear from you.

Please do visit my website https://MargaretCollins.com to see what workshops and courses are available. Do sign up, download your free ebooks or join in.

Follow me on Facebook.com/MargaretCollinsBusinessPage - I'd love to have your company.

For those who want to take their personal growth to a new level I offer coaching programmes, so do come along and find out more.

About Margaret Collins

The question "How does that work?" has inspired my career, firstly as a researcher in the biological sciences and more recently as a student of human performance and behaviour.

For more than 20 years, I have worked as a research scientist and lecturer within institutes and universities, often leading multidisciplinary teams of researchers. My primary areas of interest were in understanding just how something as small as a virus could kill something as big as us! When building my career, I saw how some people were more successful and advanced more rapidly than others – and it wasn't always related to being the brightest or the best, so I asked again "How does that work?" and that led to me training as a professional coach and in neuro-linguistic programming (NLP), cognitive behavioural coaching (CBC) and neuropsychology. I now have a diverse range of skills available to me for when I coach individual clients and groups.

I launched my career as a trainer and coach when I needed to re-create my working life to become a full-time carer for my disabled sister. The demands of a 'regular job' didn't allow me to provide the care my sister needed so I designed a more flexible life that allows me to spend more time doing things that are important to me.

For over 10 years, I have provided career and performance coaching to many clients within personal or business contexts, including many universities, small businesses and not-for-profit organisations. Combining coaching with the deep insights from NLP, CBC and neuropsychology creates opportunities for lasting change and personal development.

I provide tailored training courses and workshops in the UK and Europe and invite you to join me one day if that sounds like fun to you!

Please leave a review

Please remember that your feedback is both welcome and very helpful so I'd very much appreciate it if you would take a minute to leave review of this book on Amazon. That would be amazing.

To your journey!

Margaret

Printed in Great Britain
by Amazon